GRACE DISCOVERED

A Mother's Journey of Hope

GRACE DISCOVERED

A Mother's Journey of Hope

ANNIE E

A FAMILY RECLAMATION PROJECT PUBLICATION

Grace Discovered: A Mother's Journey of Hope
© 2016 by Annie E
gracediscovered317@gmail.com

Published by Family Reclamation Project
www.familyreclamationproject.com

ISBN: 978-1542467971

Cover Photo by Necia Clare Photography
Instagram: neciaclare
Cover Design by Sarah Ann MacPherson
Instagram: saraheisenlohr

To my sons,
whom I love and admire:
you gave me the best job in the world!

CONTENTS

FOREWORD

I've talked with women all across the country, women who had high ideals and hopes, women whose hearts and lives were dedicated to God and to their families; and time after time I heard stories of shattered dreams from mothers with broken hearts. These stories were not coming from women who had been slack in their spiritual responsibility, but rather from ones who had worked hard to pass on their faith in Jesus Christ to the next generation and especially that part of the next generation closest to their heart: their own children. The particulars of the stories varied, but the essential element was the same: one or more of their dear children had wandered from the faith and walked away from the blessed heritage they'd been given and from all they'd been taught.

My own family was not immune. As I identified with this grievous heartache, I began making a list of these mothers and their children's names. My list grew longer and longer everywhere I went. It didn't seem to matter what the church background was or what schooling choice the family had decided on or how spiritual the parents were.

In fact, some of the most spiritually keen parents were the most vulnerable. We are all aware of well-known pastors and preachers who have also struggled with this same heartbreak; among them are Billy Graham, John Piper, and Jim Cymbala.

The problem seems epidemic in our day. We are most prone to asking why and attempting to point to some parental failure. We want so much to have tidy reasons and watertight solutions. And while examination is good and necessary, trying to fix the problem is generally missing a more transcendent truth. Through her own journey with parental disillusionment and pain, Annie opens up to us an entirely different vista. She takes our hand as we walk with her through her long, dark valley—a mirror of our own—and leads us to the mountaintop where we can view the incredible love of the Father. From this vantage point we can learn to rest, to trust, to hope again. Here we lay down our striving and self-preservation and learn to wait upon God. Here the shackles that bound us fall off and we learn to walk in "the freedom for which Christ has set us free."

As I read Annie's manuscript, I came to know and love a woman I'd not yet met. She was real and vulnerable, without wallowing in self-pity. Her heart is open, sometimes raw, and we see a woman desperate to know God. But she is more than simply honest; she is humble and teachable, allowing the many gifts given to the Body of Christ to minister to her spirit.

I found myself in every chapter, yet she led me beyond myself into a deeper understanding and walk with God. She gave me a yearning to know God better and to seek Him with all my heart. It is my prayer, and I know it is hers as well, that this book will be used of God to draw you closer to Himself, to envelope you in a love that is deeper, higher, broader, longer than the pain of your personal journey, a love that "heals the broken-hearted" by pouring upon you the balm of comfort and hope, peace and even joy.

RS

ACKNOWLEDGEMENTS

I am forever grateful for the people who have walked this road with me; family and friends who often gave me hope with verses, encouraging words, and the daily support of their prayers. A special thanks to my husband's admin who believed that this project was worth attempting. She gently prodded me to write my thoughts on paper and encouraged me to its completion.

A sincere thank you to our long-lost friends in Portland, whom God brought back into our lives after a 30-year absence. What a delightful reunion! I was blessed to be a part of your lives for those few short days as you made yourselves available to help me move to the next step in this project. You became a link in a chain that would introduce me to an inspiring and thorough editor.

Rebecca, as an editor you believed in me enough to take a chance on this dream. I feel privileged to call you a friend. You seemed to have the ability to look into my heart with an uncanny understanding, helping me frame my words to better communicate the hope God has given me. My spirit felt both enriched and soothed in your presence as we pored over my manuscript, sometimes laughing, sometimes crying, sharing our stories of how God was both teaching us and walking with us in the midst of our journeys.

My dear husband, I want to thank you for your faith in me as I sought to follow God's promptings and wrote down my thoughts that slowly began to take shape and evolve into a book. It was your passionate love for God that first drew me to you, convincing me there was so much more for me to discover of God's amazing love. Thank you for affirming that I indeed had something valuable to share that could potentially encourage mothers going through similar struggles.

My sons, you are wonderful young men who inspire me with your unique talents and with your kindness and compassion. Although my joy was tempered by the perplexing and sometimes difficult teen years, it is you who helped me discover the sturdy and steadfast love of Jesus. I am genuinely grateful for the gift and privilege of being your mom.

Within the pages of this book I mention numerous authors; although not having met them in the traditional sense, they have mentored me through the pages of their writings. I am eternally indebted to them. Having been instructed, counseled, and comforted by godly men and women who put their understanding of spiritual truth into prose and poetic writing, I encourage those of you reading this narrative of my journey to further explore the discovery of God in the midst of your pain. I pray that the endnotes will be a helpful tool to guide you to authors who will point you to the hope we have in God, a hope anchored in His love for you. The healing power of Christian music and the writings of godly men and women who have walked the path before us can enable us to see the wonders of the love and grace of Father God, which fosters an increasingly joyful confidence as we learn to wait on God in prayer.

INTRODUCTION

When I was cuddling my sweet infant babies, it never crossed my mind that one of them would walk away from my passionate and my fierce mother's love for them. Not even in my most fearful imagination could I have come up with such a scenario. It simply was not on my radar screen. Not that I was a perfect mom—a fact that was not hard for me to acknowledge. Certainly, the unfinished chores, the random bickering, and the creative mischief sometimes tested my patience. However, in the busyness and craziness of raising little boys, the thought of any of my children turning their backs on our values and quite literally walking away from our home just never entered my mind. When it happened, the shock took months for me to acknowledge.

My troubled soul was equally burdened with the reality that I had always struggled with understanding and experiencing the love of God. I could easily give assent to the theological truth of God's love, even confidently citing verses to those who doubted it. However, it was not my reality. I had spent a lifetime attempting to earn God's love, trying to measure up to a standard far beyond my reach. This downward journey into a seemingly hopeless situation within our family was to be for me an epiphany of God's grace and love, a love not dependent on me but freely given nonetheless.

I have met many women struggling with similar stories and I am painfully aware that I am inadequate to counsel them as it relates to their situations. Each of our stories is unique, and any answers I would presume to give would be incomplete at best. There are many qualified people who could help you with the specifics of your journey. I only attempt to point you to God's love and wisdom that is not finite like my own. He wants to enter your story—not to simply bring a painful resolution to your circumstances, but rather to enable you to discover the hope found in the Person of Jesus, a discovery I fondly cherish.

I offer you a portion of my pursuit of God, but more importantly, God's pursuit of me. The words of James 4:8, "Draw close to God, and God will draw close to You," encapsulate my journey. When I reached out to God at my lowest point, God in His kindness met me and revealed to my broken heart His Father's heart. It is my desire that you will witness a tender, gracious God who has been working in my life to redeem the pain, using it for great good in my life. That same God passionately loves you and is waiting for you to invite Him into your most difficult of journeys.

1

BEGINNINGS...

I was sitting in a conference for pastors during my few days away, having left four young boys at home. I was trying desperately to track with a very gifted and well-known speaker. He might as well have been speaking another language as I struggled to decipher what he was saying. To my mind, this highly anticipated communicator was confusing; his presentation was random, frustrating my need for a logically laid out series of messages I could easily follow. My husband leaned over with a smile in his eyes and whispered, "How's a linear thinker like you doing?" This was, after all, a condensed opportunity to take in some much-needed nourishment to feed my weary, parched soul. Our oldest son was entering his teen years, and our youngest was just coming out of four years of asthma and related illnesses that had left me sleep deprived and exhausted.

I remember nothing the speaker shared that day except that he read from Isaiah 50:10, "If you are walking in the darkness, without a ray of light, trust in the LORD and rely on your God." In that moment it was as if God and I were alone in conversation—something I had never experienced in quite this way before; I heard Him gently whisper, "Memorize that verse." I remember reasoning, "Why? I am a stay-at-home mom to four wonderful sons, and my husband loves me. Yes, I am tired, but life is pretty good. In fact, for the most part, I love my life!" However, the urgent impression to memorize that particular verse stayed with me; so I went home, picked my favorite version of the Bible, and memorized the verse, never knowing the journey for which God was preparing me.

I felt most alive and purposeful in caring for my lively boys in spite of the exhaustion that comes from endless laundry, constant meal preparation, and countless smudges and fingerprints two to four feet up on walls and doorjambs. I had foregone furthering my education to pursue my dream of being a stay-at-home mom. It quite simply felt like I was doing what I had been created to do. The financial and educational sacrifice was a small price to pay to influence their young minds and hearts. Life was simple—no new cars, furniture, or extravagant lifestyle.

We relied on creativity and humor to help with the ups and downs of family life. And it was loads of fun! Each of our sons was dubbed with a camping name, a humorous story behind each name. Chief Frog-Catcher spent hours making a game of catching and playing with frogs. Captain Spill-Worm managed to dump the container of worms to the exasperation of his father with every attempt at teaching him the art of fishing. Sergeant

4

Trip-on-Stumpy defied any attempt at hiking by dragging his feet, with the inevitable scraped knees and hands as proof. And Private Peanut ended up in the hospital after aspirating a peanut, making for a tense and anxious night as we awaited the unavoidable surgery. Dinnertime names, Somebody, Everybody, Anybody, Nobody, were a response to "Could somebody please get the salt? Anybody? Everybody? Nobody?" My husband was quickly christened "Big Buddy" by the boys, who thought he should get in on some of the action! Games at night in our pop-up camper, four sleepy heads around the table in the morning with their steaming hot chocolate, ocean sunburns, "king of the mountain" on our floating island at the lake: they were all wonderful memories—life with a purpose.

Yet there were hints of growing restlessness as first one and then another hit adolescence. I don't remember when and where I first needed to use that directive in Isaiah 50, only that those teen years seemed to get darker and more bewildering for me with the passing of time. I still loved parenting my sons. Making cinnamon rolls and cookies for their constant stream of friends was my world. Even their many trips to the emergency room for stitches didn't faze me as I, too, had been there many times, and I felt I was in my element. But somehow as those teenage years moved on, parenting seemed less logical and more confusing. I felt increasingly responsible for the outcome of their choices, yet less influential in the choices they made. With more and more frequency, I found myself turning to that verse in Isaiah, "When you walk in the dark without a ray of light, trust in the LORD and rely on your God." (my paraphrase)

My heart longed to trust God in this darkening season, but it was so hard to trust a God who I wasn't completely convinced loved me or had a deep compassion for the accumulating pressures in our young family. His grace and love hadn't moved me deeply as of yet. I took those first steps of discovery by running to Him over and over with my fears, believing He was trustworthy even though the darkness yielded no immediate answers.

As the years rolled on, the creativity of several of my sons became channeled into teenage pranks and a propensity toward mischief and rebellion. That I could handle. I not only prayed for them with regularity, but I was also a rather good detective—or so I thought. However, I became desperate for answers when one of our sons began pulling away from our family, from our values, and, ultimately, from the faith that we espoused. Multiple phone calls were made, and advice was given; yet all the while a fog of confusion was settling in around our lives. Were there no answers that could pull him out of this downward spiral?

2

PREPARATION...

Though it didn't dawn on me at the time, in looking back I realize that God had mercifully begun preparing me for this journey. As we started down this road of confusion and desperation to save a son from a self-destructive lifestyle, I was asked to lead a women's Sunday school class. I was drawn to the subject of prayer—more specifically, prevailing prayer.

I come from a rich heritage of prayer. One of my first memories is that of seeing my dad kneeling in front of our old, scratchy blue chair, interceding for family, friends, and ministries each morning. More than once I had stood peeking around the corner in the hallway, listening for my name. Dad was too immersed in his time with his Father to know I was there. I had witnessed first-hand many answers to prayer in response to my parents' disciplined intercession; that, too, had left a deep mark on me.

So I dove into the subject of prayer with fervor. I laid out the many books from my husband's study, wonderful classics by R.A. Torrey,

Andrew Murray, and others, gleaning rich insights from them as well as from contemporary authors. Although I don't remember all those studies I wrote and shared, I was deeply impressed by the thought that God not only honors prayers but that He is also moved with compassion by our prayers. He invites us into the mystery of asking for and pursuing answers from our knees.

During my study of prayer, God clearly gave me a mission from Luke 11:5-13. In this story Jesus shared about a man who, upon the arrival of a late-night guest, turns to a friend who has already retired for the night and begs for three loaves of bread to share with his guest. Jesus comments on this man's persistence with these words:

> But I tell you this—though he won't do it for friendship's sake, if you keep knocking long enough, he will get up and give you whatever you need because of your *shameless persistence*. And so I tell you, keep on asking, and you will receive what you ask for. Keep on seeking, and you will find. Keep on knocking, and the door will be opened to you. For everyone who asks, receives. Everyone who seeks, finds. And to everyone who knocks, the door will be opened. (Luke 11:8-10, emphasis mine)

Those words became my marching orders. I could not fix our present situation with quick solutions; but I could and would keep on asking, not willing to interpret a delayed answer as a refusal.

It was around this time that my husband passed out to our congregation a little book on prayer, *The Promise of Answered Prayer* compiled by Jim Cymbala, in which the author shares a quote by Martin Luther:

> . . . ultimately, the Holy Spirit convinced me, 'No matter how you feel, you must pray! God wants you to pray, and he wants to hear your prayers—not because you are worthy, but because he is merciful.'[1]

I had yet to fully discover that this call to "shamelessly persist in prayer" was more about a compassionate, merciful God who was willing to help His children than about my constant childlike begging. However, I took Luther's directive to heart in an attempt to keep my feelings of shame and unworthiness from immobilizing me and preventing me from turning to the only One with the ultimate answers for our situation.

I remember a time in that class on prayer when I shared a compelling story told by the author Ron Mel of his visit to a friend's farm in northern California. This friend's mother would cook up a breakfast that was every young man's dream: hotcakes, fresh eggs, biscuits, and piles of sweet, smoky bacon. His description of this woman's daily encounters with God spoke deeply to me of my own need to pour out my fears and longings for my family to God. The following account is a moving portrayal of a woman profoundly aware of her dependence on God in the midst of caring for her young family, a story I read and re-read most mornings for months to follow:

> Every morning after breakfast . . . his mom would carefully stack the dishes and then disappear for an hour or so. When she came back, her eyes would be red and puffy. My friend told me this had gone on for years. When he was little, he would ask his mom where she went every day after breakfast. She would always answer, 'You wouldn't understand now, son. You're too young.'
>
> Finally, when he was a teenager, she told him what he somehow already knew. 'I just go down by the creek, sit under a cottonwood tree by myself, and talk to the Lord,' she said. 'Every day I tell Him, "There's no way in a million years I can be the wife You want me to be. There's no chance in a million worlds I can be the kind of mom You want me to be . . . unless, dear Lord, You help me."'
>
> Every morning of the world this woman would sit before the Lord by the little stream, lean her back against the rugged bark of the cottonwood, and weep out her insufficiency. And every morning of the world He would meet her and provide for her need.

Ron Mel went on to say:

It's true you know. You can't be the kind of dad or mom God wants you to be until you realize you can't be one. Then you can be one.

You can't be the man of God or the woman of God you long to be until you realize you never will be. Then you'll be closer than ever before.[2]

Like that northern California woman whose story had left a mark on me, I would daily cry out to God. Morning by morning, hour by hour, I answered alarming phone calls; attended classes with other parents who, like me, seemed punished along with their errant children; and sat across from authorities as they laid out the consequences for my son's behavior. Easy answers were not coming. But more than just learning to pray, I would soon learn that this was the beginning of my journey to know and experience firsthand the love and compassion of the God to whom I prayed.

3

PROMISES ... AND WAITING

The discovery of God in this unfolding crisis was not unlike the beginnings of my dating relationship with my husband. In those first months of dating, I discovered a witty humor, creativity in abundance, a refreshing passion for God, and many more qualities that drew me to him. As the turmoil in our home deepened and I turned to God in panic and desperation, God graciously began speaking to me, revealing so many facets of His character and personality.

I heard the voice of God out of the pages of His Word, many of the verses coming from the book of Isaiah. Through these verses God pointed me to Himself, and I felt compelled to write them down in a little black leather book, a place of reassurance to turn to on the days when fear screamed and God seemed silent. Isaiah 64:4 was the second entry in my journal of God's whisperings: "For since the world began, no ear has heard, and no eye has seen a God like you, who works for those who wait for him!"

"He works while I wait on Him!" What a comforting promise. We were not alone; God was present with us in this terrifying season. He was asking me—which would take months to permeate my soul—to transition the focus of my thoughts from the answers I longed for to a God who was good and powerful enough to actually honor His promises. In His incredible patience, verse by verse, promise by promise, I began to see this God as He actually revealed Himself in His Word rather than through my pre-conceived grid. God was promising to work; my part was to wait for Him. How many times I prayed that verse back to God, claiming its promise to me personally: "No ear has heard, and no eye has seen a God like You, and *You* promise *You are working* as I wait for You."

As the days got darker, the verses continued jumping out of the pages of Isaiah. It was at this time I read a little book, *The Life God Blesses.* In a chapter entitled "The Last Half Hour," the author Jim Cymbala makes the following comment:

> There is an ever-present tension between the greatness of his promises and the still-unchanged situations we face after we pray. . . . Herein lies the battle of faith—to hold on and keep believing God despite what our natural senses tell us. Our challenge is to wait in faith for the day of God's favor and salvation.[3]

I remember one particular day when I was again terrified for our son's future, waves of fear washing over me as I grasped the enormity of our situation and my seeming helplessness. God challenged me to go back to my journal and circle the word "*wait*" around all the promises I had been recording in recent weeks. I was amazed! Here are a few:

> For since the world began, no ear has heard, and no eye has seen a God like you, who works for those who **wait** for him! (Isaiah 64:4)

> So the LORD must **wait** for you to come to him so he can show you his love and compassion. For the LORD is a faithful God. Blessed are those who **wait** for his help. (Isaiah 30:18)

> Yet those who **wait** for the LORD will gain new strength; They will mount up with wings like eagles, they will run and not get tired, they will walk and not become weary.
> (Isaiah 40:31 NASB77)

> The LORD is wonderfully good to those who **wait** for him, to those who seek for him. It is good both to hope and **wait** quietly for the salvation of the LORD.
> (Lamentations 3:25-26 TLB)

> Be still in the presence of the LORD, and **wait** patiently for him to act.
> (Psalm 37:7)

I **waited** patiently for the LORD to help me, and he turned to me and heard my cry. He lifted me out of the pit of despair, out of the mud and the mire. He set my feet on solid ground and steadied me as I walked along. He has given me a new song to sing, a hymn of praise to our God. Many will see what he has done and be amazed. They will put their trust in the LORD. (Psalm 40:1-3)

Looking back on those fear-filled days, I realize that waiting on God was part of His plan. Not only was God teaching me to face my complete and utter dependence on Him for answers for our sons; but also, in the waiting, His presence was imperceptibly changing me. Although I continued to ask shamelessly for His divine intervention, my heart began to open to the wonder of a Creator who loved me.

One of the gifts God gave me was sending a dear friend into my life who had walked this lonely journey with her son a few years prior to my own story. Only recently we talked of the panic and desperation that had marked our conversations as she quietly sought to remind me of God's faithfulness.

As I look back, I realized that *I* was holding God to His promises as a right I had to claim rather than living with the awareness that *God* had made promises to me because, in fact, He dearly loved me. I am ashamed to say that I longed for God to fix my broken life more than I longed for

Him. That longing was changing through the long, lonely months and years of waiting on God. In His kindness God continued to reveal His heart through His many promises.

As the weeks and months rolled on, there was a point in time in this long dark tunnel when I became aware that God did, in fact, love *me*, a concept I had struggled with most of my Christian life. This awakening in my heart to God's love came about shortly before our son turned eighteen. A free spirit ready to travel, without money, without divulging a clear plan, he left with no assurance that he would ever look back.

On a cold wintry day, I read the words of yet another promise that brought warmth to my broken heart. God's exiled children cried out in Isaiah 49:14, 15: "The LORD has deserted us; the LORD has forgotten us." To their cry God responded, "Never! Can a mother forget her nursing child? Can she feel no love for the child she has borne? But even if that were possible, I would not forget you!"

God's love for me was greater than any love I could possibly have for my son. It wasn't possible that I could do anything but feel the weight of anxiety night and day. Thoughts and fears for him lay at every level of my conscious and unconscious thoughts. And yet God said that even if it were humanly possible for me to forget my son and move on with my life, He would not forget me. Amazing: God's love for me—deeper than my love for my son?

I shared this new discovery with my husband. I remember him asking with curiosity, "You're not having trouble with the love of God anymore, are you?" For the first time in my life I could honestly answer that I knew and actually felt God's love. It was through the deepest aching of a mother's heart for her son that I could finally understand God's love for His children, more specifically, for me! Shortly thereafter, my husband surprised me with a bracelet engraved with the words from Isaiah 49:15, *"I will not forget you"*—a turning point in my life, now etched on a simple silver bracelet, a reminder of the moment I began to understand this profound Truth: God loves me!

By reflecting over and over on these promises that filled my journal, my focus was changing from simply crying out for the answers I craved to a growing longing for a God who was waiting to reveal His love for me. He had my attention!

4

BROKENNESS

In the infancy of the crisis with our son, overwhelmed with fear and the enormity of our situation, I prayed a simple yet desperate prayer: "If I have to go through this, don't let me go unchanged. Please don't let these tears be wasted." God heard and responded quickly.

Shortly after I offered up this prayer of surrender to God, I went into our local bank to request their help in acquiring a cash card for our son who was eager and ready to leave. His chosen destination for beginning his new life was a mere thousand miles away. There appeared to be no forethought or any planned means of returning home. He was comfortable with the idea of hitchhiking; I definitely wasn't! We were simply attempting to find a way to replenish a card if he found himself in a crisis situation or with a change of heart and a desire to return home. So in a bit of fear-motivated panic, I found myself trying to explain my situation and what exactly I wanted to a very gracious, but baffled, middle-aged woman at our bank.

Feeling a bit flustered and wanting to keep our circumstances private, I was having a hard time communicating what I specifically needed. After a few minutes of a rather confusing exchange, she gently asked about the nature of our situation so that she could better assist me. Somewhat humiliated, I briefly explained. I was not prepared for her quick and vulnerable response. She began telling me of her daughter who had made the same choices. "How are you surviving?" she inquired with visible sincerity. I simply responded that I could never walk this journey apart from my faith and my relationship with Jesus. It was a short conversation, but a profound reminder of the prayer I had offered to God to not let my tears be wasted. Here was the beginning of God's answer: an opportunity to speak of God's faithfulness.

Even as I hoped for something good to come out of this painfully long season—perhaps the opportunity to help other struggling mothers who walked a similar road—that frantic prayer I lifted up to God would only scratch the surface of the discoveries that would unfold. I subsequently ran across a quote by Ravi Zacharias that gave new direction to my prayer:

> At the end of your life one of three things will happen to your heart: it will grow hard, it will be broken, or it will be tender. Nobody escapes. Your heart will become coarse and desensitized, be crushed under the weight of disappointment, or be made

tender by that which makes the heart of God tender.[4]

God was tenderizing my heart and brokenness was His tool, sensitizing me to the hurting world around me and to the magnitude of His love for me.

I so related to Jared Wilson's depiction of this journey in his book *Gospel Wakefulness*. The condition he coins as "gospel wakefulness," that is, "treasuring Christ more greatly and savoring His power more sweetly,"[5] he explains, comes in two subsequent steps: "be utterly broken, and be utterly awed."[6] In the chapter that follows, entitled "Nonnegotiable Brokenness," he articulates well the description of this pathway of discovery when he says,

> . . . gospel wakefulness comes at the intersection of personal brokenness and the gospel. For many Christians a perfect storm of personal emptiness and the fullness of Christ is brewing. . . . The way to the joy of gospel wakefulness is personal brokenness—it always has been.[7]

I found it difficult to know where to place this chapter as that "perfect storm" had been taking shape measured by months and years rather than by days or hours. My declining confidence in my parenting skills was being chipped away by thoughtless words from well-meaning observers, who for the most part were only trying to help, and by the recognition that I was relying on the opinion and affirmation of others to define my worth. Consequently, my eyes were opening to the realization of idols—those things I trusted in rather than in God alone—idols that needed to be smashed. These idols and the accompanying emptiness that was their companion were appearing like vague shadows in the early morning dawn, long before the rising sun brings sharpness and definition to the landscape. But they were taking shape, nonetheless, with increasing clarity.

In spite of my emotional pain and fear in this darkening season, I began allowing God to reveal to me those crutches upon which I was leaning so heavily and the abundance of tangled motives deeply embedded in my heart. God opened my eyes to the truth that all was not well with my soul. Why was I was so distraught and devastated by insinuations of disapproval by people whose opinion of me I highly valued? Was their perception of my value based on their assessment of my performance as a parent? Had I leaned on these judgments to define my worth? Definitely! Words of praise were like a balm, first to the wounds of a little girl, and now to those of a young woman, who was craving for words of affirmation to be spoken over her. At no point was it more valuable and meaningful than in my parenting; at no point was I more vulnerable to the temptation to trust in something other than God to give me worth.

I remember sitting in a restaurant with our four little boys when an elderly couple stopped to comment on our beautiful, well-behaved little family. They opened their wallet and handed each of our sons a dollar to reward them for their good manners. I had spent a lifetime of depending on good behavior. For the first half of my life, I had depended on my own good behavior to define me; and now my self-definition was, in part, dependent on my sons' behavior.

Over the span of months and even years, with a process I can only define as brokenness, God continued to chip away those false gods that had held me in such seemingly good stead for so many years. With gentleness He drew me to Jesus, to the revelation of Himself that came alive in the pages of His Word, to the compassion that moved Him to reach down to me in my awkward attempts to reach up to Him.

Something profound was happening in me. My heart, which for so much of my life had lacked any affection for God, was gradually being made tender by His love. I could relate to Jared Wilson's description of this process when he says, "The greater the brokenness, the greater the impulse to trust him. The greater the trust in him, the greater the joy. . . ."[8] The process of breaking was pressing me to Jesus, and in Jesus I was finding the birthing of joy in the ever-increasing glimpses of His love and grace for me. It left me in awe.

I never wanted brokenness to dead end in me—something God used exclusively for my benefit. I didn't even covet it for the additional benefit of helping others. I longed for brokenness to open my distant heart to the glorious awareness of God's love and grace and to the discovery that God is truly enough. The motivation for helping others began to come from the overflow of God meeting me in my pain. I was humbled by the increasing awareness that I had so little to offer to the hurting world around me, yet God was continually bringing people into my life to speak His love into their bruised and fragile lives.

Daily my desperate prayer to not let my tears be wasted was being answered. God was intersecting my life at the point of brokenness, leaving me forever changed. However, this change did not happen overnight; it came in increments. Brokenness would become a theme, a tool God would use, layered through all He would be teaching me on the path that lay ahead.

5

DARKNESS

Not only were we dealing with the daily stresses and complexities of attempting to rescue our son, but I was also facing a new enemy I had never encountered before: A creeping depression had invaded my heart. I had not appreciated all that one faces in the throes of a sadness so deep it awakened me at night in a sweaty panic and of a fear so intense it sent me racing to the phone to pray with my sister, many times too choked with sobs to pray myself.

God in His compassion met me at every turn as He was opening my heart to His Word, sending comforters to continuously point me not only to His answers but also to the compassionate, gracious God who gave them. My sister-in-law shared verses with me, which I wrote on little pieces of notebook paper, placing them in my pocket to take out and memorize during the day. Some of the verses I had written, using a combination of several versions, were found in 2 Corinthians 1:8b-11:

We were crushed and overwhelmed beyond our ability to endure, and we thought we would never live through it. In fact we expected to die [ESV—Indeed, we felt that we had received the sentence of death.] But as a result, we stopped relying on ourselves and learned to rely only on God, who raised the dead. And he did rescue us from mortal danger, [ESV—He delivered us from such a deadly peril] and he will rescue us again. We have placed our confidence in him, and he will continue to rescue us. And you are helping us by praying for us. Then many people will give thanks because God has graciously answered so many prayers for our safety.

I identified with Paul; I felt crushed and overwhelmed beyond my ability to endure. This grueling season felt like a death sentence. I remember the day my husband unsuspectingly picked up a little wadded-up piece of torn paper from my dresser with that verse meticulously written on it, thinking it was garbage. I panicked. I needed that verse. It was my lifeline to get through yet another day of wrestling with my thoughts and fears.

I had not spent a lot of wasted energy questioning God or being wrapped up in self-condemnation, but on one particular day I found myself falling prey to Satan's taunts as I drove alone down the main thoroughfare through our small city. As I pulled up to a stoplight in front of a local grocery store, in my spirit I heard a voice clearly say, *"You are such a loser"*—words *I* had certainly never said or used. I remember turning around and looking to see who had spoken. No one was with me; I was completely alone in my van! In my spirit God spoke the words, *"That wasn't Me."* He continued with the words from Romans 8:1 that I had memorized from my childhood, *"There is no condemnation to those who are in Christ Jesus."* In that moment I saw myself as God saw me. I was not the mom defined by four teenage sons, nor even the woman defined as the pastor's wife. I was the child of God in whom God saw His Son, and He did not condemn me; He loved me.

This concept was to be revolutionary for me although I felt like I was only skirting the fringes of this truth. I was discovering that I unknowingly was defining myself by how others perceived my weaknesses and strengths, and by how significant people in my life viewed my children. In some ways I had been here before. Being a twin, I had spent years defining myself by the constant comparisons that marked my identity. Yet here I was again, placing people and their opinions in a position higher than God's declared value of me. This false, inaccurate self-evaluation made me an easy target for Satan's lies and deception.

I found Peter's pointed warning playing again and again in my mind: "Be watchful. Your adversary the devil prowls around like a roaring lion, seeking someone to devour."(1 Peter 5:8 ESV) Just as Satan's lies randomly taunted me in this long dark winter, so also the Holy Spirit repeatedly brought Peter's solemn admonition to my mind to counter those attacks.

On yet another occasion as I pulled up to a stoplight on my way to work, I was haunted by the recurring thought that my son's choices were somehow my fault. Maybe if I had been more aware, more tuned in, I could have stopped this escalating spiral in our son. I was overcome with regrets, and I struggled to see through my tears as I drove those last few miles.

I breathed a prayer for help. Hoping for some words of encouragement, I turned on a Christian radio station and caught the closing words of a well-known Christian counselor speaking on the topic of teenage rebellion. He presented three factors that influence their behavior: their environment, their personality, and their choices. I don't know that these three factors are all inclusive, but I do know that I heard a message God had for me at that moment.

As the counselor expanded and developed the subject of teenage rebellion, it was as if a heavy fog momentarily lifted. I was acutely aware that I could not control all these factors, and I'd been arrogant to somehow think I could; I grasped the truth that I was only a part of the equation. Satan was again using guilt, feelings of failure, and an unhealthy introspection to immobilize me. I was in a battle and I needed to focus on the mission God had given me: to use my influence as best I could and to "ask and keep on asking." (Luke 11:9) My hope was in God, not in the illusion that maybe

I could fix this messy situation. So once again I turned to Him.

Satan was indeed stalking, prowling, and waiting to pounce on me when I was most vulnerable. He is both cunning and resourceful; therefore, I often found I was blindsided by his attacks. He would subtly feed my doubts and fears and then hit when I was weak and at an emotionally low point. Yet God, ever-present and gracious, continually provided me with rays of hope in my dark life.

My memory takes me to one wintry day when my spirit matched the cold, bleak northwestern winter. I was simultaneously grieving the loss of my dad and the close relationship I had shared with my parents in our sons' pre-teenage years, as well as the apparent loss of our son. I struggled to define what, in particular, on any given day I was grieving. Maybe, I reasoned, if I could identify my grief, it would bring clarity to my tangled emotions.

It was on such a gloomy day I got a rare call from my brother. I seldom even knew what part of the world he was in as his job in missions would often take him overseas. This made his call an even more pointed miracle. The purpose of his call was to simply give me the following verse: "You keep track of all my sorrows. You have collected all my tears in your bottle. You have recorded each one in your book." (Psalm 56:8)

I hung onto that verse. It was one of those verses that ended up in my pocket, daily reminding me that God sees my tears and my grief. My sorrow needs no explanation to His waiting ears; He is a compassionate God, tracking my every tear. Wow!

I ran across a quote of Martyn Lloyd-Jones in Jared Wilson's book, *Gospel Wakefulness*, which gave me some perspective in this battle with depression from the viewpoint of a Psalm writer: "Why am I discouraged? Why is my heart so sad? I will put my hope in God! I will praise him again—my Savior and my God!" (Psalm 42:11) Like the psalmist, Martyn Lloyd-Jones asks the question, "Have you realized that most of your unhappiness in life is due to the fact that you are listening to yourself instead of talking to yourself?" I certainly had been guilty of that. My heart on any given day was a cauldron of guilt, fear, remorse, and a host of other varied emotions that rolled through my mind like thunderheads on a summer afternoon, demanding my attention. Martyn Lloyd-Jones continues,

> You have to take yourself in hand, address yourself, preach to yourself, question yourself . . . and say to yourself: 'Hope thou in God' . . . And then you must go on to remind yourself of God, who God is, and what God is and what God has done, and what God has pledged to do.[9]

Rather than listen to myself and entertain my fears, I am to call myself to hope in God. I am to remind myself that I will praise Him again, a task made easier when, even in the midst of my depression, I see His kindness visiting our situa-

tion again and again. Jared Wilson sums it up well
with a statement by John Stott:

> The cure for spiritual depression is neither
> to look in at our grief, nor back to the past,
> nor round at our problems, but away and
> up to the living God. He is our help and our
> God, and if we trust in him now, we shall
> soon have cause to praise him again.[10]

Although Satan would tempt me to look inward
with blame and to look at an unknown future with
fear, God was graciously helping me to look up
and discover a God who was "my Savior" and "my
God."

Like the lesson learned by the psalm writer
David, trusting in my own skills and resources had
caused me to come up short. David says it best
when from Psalm 33 he states with confidence:

> The best-equipped army cannot save a
> king, nor is great strength enough to save a
> warrior. Don't count on your warhorse to
> give you victory—for all its strength, it
> cannot save you. But the LORD watches
> over those who fear him, those who rely
> on his unfailing love. He rescues them
> from death and keeps them alive in times
> of famine. We put our hope in the LORD. *He*
> is our help and our shield. In him our
> hearts rejoice, for we trust in his holy
> name. Let your unfailing love surround us,
> LORD, for our hope is in *you alone*. (Psalm
> 33:16-22, emphases mine)

6

FRIENDS AND OTHERWISE

I have always struggled a bit too keenly with feeling people's disapproval. I was especially sensitive to how our church was feeling about our wayward son, now gone from home, his situation deteriorating.

On one particular Sunday, between our two morning worship services, I had been visiting with a young man my husband had mentored through some troubling and difficult years. He had returned to town for the weekend; and oddly enough, I have not seen him since this brief encounter which left such a deep mark on me. He, like so many others, asked how our son was doing. Choosing my words carefully and always choosing with caution those with whom I would share, I simply responded with a short, evasive answer.

What he said next had a profound effect on me. With indifference he said, "You don't have to tell me anything, 'so-and-so' has already filled me in on all the details." And with those callous words he walked into the sanctuary. I was speechless! Angry! The singing had already begun; and as I stood alone in the foyer, a battle ensued in my mind. Everything in me wanted to walk out the door and head home. I wanted to reject the church and to believe the lie Satan had taunted me with in my teen years: Christians were indeed all a "bunch of hypocrites." I had come to that abrupt conclusion many years before as I witnessed zealous "Christians" whose words had not matched their actions, whose bold witness was accompanied by a mocking cruelty.

Now, here in the present, I was confronted with the irony that the person who had passed on this information was one with whom I had not personally shared. What now? Although the lies were pounding in my ears, I began to hear the gentle whisper of Jesus, "We can do this; I will go in there with you. You are not alone!" Satan's taunting immediately stopped as I took, what for me, was a giant step of faith. I entered that sanctuary—not alone, but with the acute awareness that Jesus and I were doing this together.

I share this story not to relive the loneliness that was my frequent companion in this season or to stir up the bitterness in which I was tempted to indulge, but to say that there were varying responses to our family's upheaval that compounded my grief. For many, it must have been uncomfortable to have the pastor's family in crisis. I watched friendships drift away. In an attempt to cope with our ever-challenging and ever-changing fragile circumstances, I found myself withdrawing.

We were in crisis maintenance mode with little energy or reserves left for others. I lost friends who were irritated and hurt that I wasn't there for them; they easily reinvested their energies in relationships with more to offer. Others were bold enough to ask for "all the details" so they could "pray." Still others would comment with frequency, "I'm here for you if you ever need to talk." That might sound benign, or like I am simply being trivial; but when battling depression, the weight of being the initiator in relationships is a very heavy and unwanted load to bear.

As God began to pull me out of that dark night, I wondered and was even angered that some friends never asked, "Is everything OK? Haven't heard from you in a while; how are you doing?" Was there some expectation that as their pastor's wife I was somehow immune from experiencing emotions? Was I to perform roles and fulfill expectations that were as varied as the people who attended our church? More than likely, without the crisis in view, many had simply moved on. Most were not even aware that our son was miles from home, where we rarely knew his location. Their insensitivity was a thorn to me.

However, in the midst of these troubling relationships, God graciously gave me comforters. Many of these friendships surprised me and grew deep during those tough years. The following stories give a glimpse of God's gentle touch on my life through His people.

Shortly after a crisis with our son that I feared would end our ministry, I walked into a prayer time that preceded our *DivorceCare.* I was not involved in this ministry, but my husband had encouraged me to stop by to connect with the team. I dreaded questions and small talk, yet somehow on that particular evening I felt compelled to drop in. A couple that had known and served with us for years pulled me aside and shared a verse that God had given them for us from the book of Isaiah:

> I have called you back from the ends of the earth so you can serve me. For I have chosen you and will not throw you away. Don't be afraid, for I am with you. Do not be dismayed, for I am your God. I will strengthen you and help you. I will hold you up with my victorious right hand. (Isaiah 41:9, 10)

God had drawn me there that night because He had a message for me. He was not discarding us! How timely! This couple continued to take us to dinner every three or four months just to check up on us, sensitive to the ongoing burden we carried.

I was also deeply moved by another God-sent friendship that came from a widow around my age, who, although losing her husband to cancer, was repeatedly sensitive to the needs in my life. It humbled me as I had so little to offer her in this dark season. Because God had used the devotional *Streams in the Desert* to build my faith and give me hope, I gave her a copy. It became our habit in the early morning hours to text back and forth verses and thoughts shared by devotional writers from the distant past written within the pages of this little book. This habit went on for months as we sought to encourage each other and bring one another before our loving Father. What a role model she became for me.

During this time God brought into my life two women whose lives were also thrown into upheaval by children who had made destructive choices. One of these women, only with me for two short years before her husband's career moved them on, spent hours helping me care for a very assertive, intimidating woman dying of cancer whom God had placed in my life. Although I had a deep burden to share Christ with this gravely ill woman, I found it too daunting a task to care for and meet with her on my own. I was raw with grief myself and felt void of words to give comfort and hope. Yet the burden I carried for her was inescapable. Others had simply written her off, and I remember how hard I looked to find someone willing to help me as I knew I could not go it alone. I asked this new acquaintance if she would be willing to help. Surprisingly, with little or no hesitancy, she agreed.

My new friend and I spent many hours caring for this woman tortured by a horrendous and abusive past. Those hours together gave us many moments in which to share our lives and our stories. She encouraged me and gave me hope that God was not finished working in our son's life. Her quiet demeanor and confidence in God was infectious, and I knew their military assignment was a divine appointment both for our dying friend and for my wounded heart.

Another woman, a part of the life group that we attend, texts me to this day, faithfully checking up on our sons, wondering how she can pray. Her sincerity and sensitivity, never judging or questioning, has given me an open place to share. There was a time in the thick of our crisis when most of the participants in our life group were struggling with a challenging young adult child. Was this a coincidence? I think not! God had placed us together in a loving community to be fellow comforters, to live out Paul's description in 2 Corinthians 1:4: "He comforts us in all our troubles so that we can comfort others. When they are troubled, we will be able to give them the same comfort God has given us."

Although there continued to be some random insensitivity to our situation within the Christian community, I discovered role models as well who taught me the delicate balance of loving those in pain. To me they were glimpses of Jesus, hands and hearts I long to emulate.

7

DOUBTS

I had always been terrified of the phone call I feared would come, the call telling me that my son was in trouble far from home. When it came, our life was thrown into a whirlwind. I couldn't get over the physical feeling that I had just been punched in the stomach, so strong was my anxiety and fear.

We felt impressed by God that we were to go—a trip we knew God was in as He provided a succession of miracles to make it possible. However, after an agonizing two days of seeing our son and visiting with authorities at various levels, I was exhausted and emotionally spent.

Minutes after getting back to our hotel room, we received a brief call from my husband's district superintendent. Although he was gracious and supportive, I felt angry and vulnerable. Once again we were parenting in a fishbowl. At a low moment in my confidence in God, I sarcastically remarked to my husband, "So, what else can go wrong?" Before the words were out of my mouth, the phone rang. Another son had hit a deer with our van a few miles from home. "Really God?" I picked up my Bible and it literally fell open to Isaiah 48. I glanced down and verses 10-11 jumped out of the pages at me:

> . . . I have refined you in the furnace of suffering. I will rescue you for my sake—yes, for my own sake! That way the pagan nations will not be able to claim that their gods have conquered me. I will not let them have my glory!

Wow, God! You came through with a word of promise! You are in this! Immediately, I sensed God's peace and presence. I wanted to honor God as He exhorted Asaph in Psalm 50:15 when He said, "Then call on me when you are in trouble, and I will rescue you, and you will give me glory."

My cynical attitude evaporated as I recognized God was in even this situation. I simply wrote, "Rescue us for your name's sake, Father!" He had not abandoned us. He was not going to waste this grief. As I looked over my journal, the immediate entries that preceded it read:

> I am holding you by your right hand—I, the LORD your God. And I say to you, 'Do not be afraid. I am here to help you.'
> (Isaiah 41:13)

> For the Lord does not abandon anyone forever. Though he brings grief, he also shows compassion according to the greatness of his unfailing love.
> (Lamentations 3:31-32)

When you go through deep waters and great trouble, I will be with you. When you go through rivers of difficulty, you will not drown. When you walk through the fire of oppression, you will not be burned up; the flames will not consume you. For I am the LORD, your God, the Holy One of Israel, your Savior.
(Isaiah 43:2-3a)

I was amazed with all these whisperings of God. I had never experienced anything like this before. There seemed to be no specific pattern or timing. Those moments were so spontaneous, so surprising; and yet there He was, addressing the deep needs of my soul in the moment. I often thought it would have been much easier to go through this season with a checklist, feeling like I had mastered a concept, a trial, before I moved on to tackle the next one. But somehow that would have seemed so strangely impersonal. Instead, God reached out to me on a daily basis as the fears and failures surfaced, revealing to me different facets of His character, teaching me to lean on Him.

My struggles surfaced randomly. Sometimes the struggles were with issues of faith; sometimes, with the loneliness of alienation; sometimes, with immense feelings of failure. But God faithfully met me, opening to me His heart of love and healing. He was working in so many areas of my life, meeting me in the moment. At times it seemed almost amusing how God counseled me in the oddest places. More often than not, He spoke words of comfort on that main drag through our little town on my way home from work.

After a few hours at work, my undisciplined mind would frequently roam to places I knew it shouldn't go, resulting in an overwhelming feeling of despair. As I got in my car to head home, I would turn on the Christian radio station and offer up a tearful prayer begging to hear from God. In His great compassion, Father God would have a song or a speaker prepared for me.

I remember on more than one occasion, with tears rolling down my face, singing along with the group Among the Thirsty the chorus of "I'd Need a Savior." There is something so very soothing in singing the name of Jesus over and over again; I was reminding myself that Jesus is not only there for me in the bleakest of nights as my Savior, but He is also ever-present with me as my Counselor and Friend.

Another time God touched my soul with the sweet words from Sanctus Real, "Whatever You're Doing":

> *Whatever You're doing inside of me*
> *It feels like chaos, but I believe . . .*
> *You're up to something bigger than me,*
> *Larger than life,*
> *Something heavenly, something heavenly.*[11]

God was working in me. This pain had purpose. He not only wanted to work in my sons, but He was also stirring something in me, something that would not be accomplished overnight. Through tearfully learning to walk with Him in this season, I was finding that "the one who is in you is greater than the one who is in the world" (1 John 4:4, NIV). Amazingly, every time Satan showed up, God did as well. The lies I had entertained for a lifetime were slowly being replaced with the truth of God's love for me.

8

SHERRIE

The short description we have of Enoch in Genesis 5 has always aroused a certain curiosity and fascination in me. Simply put it says, "Enoch walked with God." Was this trial teaching me, by virtue of the desperate situation we were facing through days and nights of paralyzing fear, that hanging on to God was to be a new norm for me? Although I could see no answers to my cries for help nor an immediate resolution to the web that had been spun by a reckless and fearless son, this new "walking with God" was providing numerous moments of tangible encouragement. On almost a daily basis God was speaking to my tangled thoughts and feelings and to my deepest fears with amazing gentleness.

As I began discovering the joy and intimacy of walking with Him, He continually reassured me of His love for our son. By listening to His whisperings, I saw with increasing clarity the evidence of God's involvement in the circumstances of my life. It might be a song, an unexpected encouragement from a friend, or an impression from God. Such was the miracle of Sherrie.

On one particular night I awoke from a deep sleep with the words embedded in my mind, "Call..."—and then God specified a location I was to call! There was a deep sense of urgency that did not leave me as I lay awake in the predawn hours. I never doubted that God was indeed speaking to me, and I spent the remainder of the night attempting to make sense of the instructions as I prayed my way to the sunrise.

Oddly, I didn't know why or to whom I was making this call, only that it had something to do with ongoing paperwork for the consequences of our son's poor choices. I had been muddling through paperwork with my son for months. He was so discouraged with the unreturned phone calls and the constant rudeness with which he was treated that he was giving up.

Knowing the long-term importance of follow-through, I had offered to help. It was with this backdrop and with a great deal of apprehension I placed that call. I discovered, much to my deep dismay, that there was indeed another impending crisis, this one due to bureaucratic sloppiness— lost paperwork. There was absolutely no way to resolve it in less than twenty-four hours. Without a quick resolution, our son faced severe consequences.

Backed into a corner, God provided a miracle, a woman named Sherrie. I was quite used to the run-around: being put on hold, being disconnected, being shuffled back and forth between departments. Rudeness seemed to be the order of the day in this harried and impersonal office. However, on this day a woman named Sherrie answered my call. She simply and kindly and so uncharacteristically stated that she could help me. For one entire day we sent faxes back and forth and resolved the crisis.

What so deeply touches me about God's compassion and lovingkindness is that in all my subsequent calls I could never locate Sherrie. No one seemed to know of or about anyone with the name Sherrie. I'm looking forward to discovering the nature of this "Sherrie" someday, but for now I'm grateful to God for His kindness to us.

Lamentations 3:22-26 had already been precious to me in this season but was even more so now:

> The unfailing love of the LORD never ends!
> . . . Great is his faithfulness, his mercies begin afresh each day. . . . The LORD is wonderfully good to those who wait for him.

So ended another day of walking with God with yet a further reminder that He loved us.

9

HAWAII

I have struggled with shame most of my life, though I'm not actually sure where and when its insidious roots became so deeply embedded in my soul. As a child I was motivated into a relationship with God primarily to stay out of hell; as a teenager my motivation was elevated to that of service for God, a seemingly honorable desire out of which to relate to God. But what about *love* for God? It seemed illusive, something I could not conjure up. Many verses were deeply embedded in my heart from childhood, but what seemed to surface were verses of instruction or promises for the obedient. Always a sense of guilt and shame was driving my relationship with God.

My awareness of God's love has definitely been a journey. Previously I had glimpses of His love amidst a nondescript life of attempted service for God. Because my Christian life had been defined more by *my* actions rather than by God's, I have concluded that brokenness and long periods of waiting were necessary catalysts in order to discover the warmth of His love. Brokenness became my friend as it required me to wait on a God I felt I barely knew. My words exhausted and my actions ineffective in this period of heartbreak, I often could only repeat the words over and over taught to me by none other than Martin Luther, "Lord, have mercy." And mercy God gave, minute by minute, prayer by prayer.

Into this long painful season, God gave my husband his dream vacation, a trip for the two of us to Hawaii. This vacation was made possible through gifts from a couple very sensitive to our spiritual needs and from a son who shared his tax return, money that could have easily been put to other uses by a cash-strapped college student who knew and used every dollar menu in his university town. Because of their kindness I was provided not only with rest, adventures, and hours of endless sun, but also with a meeting alone with God every morning that forever changed my view of Him.

Each morning I would set my alarm for 5:30 and head out in the dark to walk the beach and talk to God, relishing the beauty of His creation that I was privileged to share. As the sun rose over the mountains bordering the island, it would first cast its glow on the top of the clouds, turning them a brilliant pink while the horizon was still lost in the shadows of predawn. It mesmerized me each morning as I stopped at the same spot to worship my Creator and enjoy His beauty.

It was during those early morning strolls on the beaches of Maui that I first discovered sea glass—broken, discarded glass that had been tumbled by the ocean and turned into beautiful little pebbles that filled my pockets each morning. But there was more beauty to be discovered.

Beyond the wonder of creation was the wonder of the Creator Himself beckoning me. After wandering the beach, I returned to our hotel and headed out to the balcony of our room with my coffee and the book *The Singing God*, by Sam Storms. A dear friend had given me the gift of Zephaniah 3:17 on my son's eighteenth birthday, ironically only days before he left home on his search to discover his world. Zephaniah 3:17 reads:

> For the LORD your God is living among you. He is a mighty savior. He will take delight in you with gladness. With his love, he will calm all your fears. He will rejoice over you with joyful songs.

It was on this dream vacation several years later that God used this verse along with this book to reframe my life each morning as I sat on that balcony reading, allowing His love to wash over me. Chapter after chapter I discovered how God related to me. My response was overwhelming love, love I no longer felt I must attempt to conjure up.

I was particularly moved that God would "rejoice over me with joyful songs." Shame I understood; someone rejoicing over me, I did not. Unfortunate words had been spoken over me during this dark season that left me with deep wounds. As I read of a God who saves me, and even delights in me, those wounds—and even their scars—were healing in a mysterious way.

In his chapter "Orphans to Heirs" Sam Storms draws an amazing analogy of God not only as a judge who saves us from the penalty of our sins, but also as a father who chooses to adopt us. Equally fascinating was his description of adoption in the ancient world, a process driven by very different motivations from our present day adoptions. Sam Storms quotes J. I. Packer's insightful description of the adoption process in the following:

> Adoption was a practice ordinarily confined to the childless well-to-do. Its subjects . . . were not normally infants . . . but young adults who had shown themselves fit and able to carry on a family name in a worthy way. In this case, however, God adopts us out of free love, not because our character and record show us worthy to bear His name, but despite the fact that they show the very opposite. We are not fit for a place in God's family; the idea of His loving and exalting us as He loves and has exalted the Lord Jesus sounds ludicrous and wild—yet that, and nothing less than that, is what our adoption means.[12]

This picture of adoption was profound and bore new implications for me. My adoption into God's family is not based on my worthiness as was the recipient of adoption in ancient Palestine. It is not earned based on how well I perform for my

Master; I have not in some way proven myself worthy of being called His child. My adoption is based entirely on God and His great love for me. It is something He did for me, not something I earned from Him.

Sam Storms summed up both justification and adoption when he painted this picture:

> When you are justified by faith in Christ, you stand before God as Judge and hear Him declare, 'Not guilty! Righteous through faith in Jesus!' Praise God! But in adoption, God the Judge steps down from behind His legal bench, removes His stately robes, stoops down, and takes you into His arms of love, saying softly, 'My son, my daughter, my child!'[13]

As much as the doctrine of justification would move me in the months to come, the concept of adoption stirred me deeply in those quiet moments alone with God. In the stillness of the early morning with worries and voices separated by an ocean, I could hear God's quiet voice as He spoke to me of His love. He not only paid the price of death demanded of sinners who reject their Creator; He went still further and adopted me. Because I had keenly felt that human love was forever attached to my performance, this love had proven imperfect and disappointing; but I now was experiencing a love that was not dependent on *me*. As His adopted child, I was discovering a God who loves me because He *is* love.

Though difficult to wrap my mind around, another enlightening quote by J. I. Packer shared within the pages of this chapter overwhelmed me with this equally profound thought:

> God receives us as sons, and loves us with the same steadfast affection with which He eternally loves His beloved only begotten. There are no distinctions of affection in the divine family. We are all loved just as fully as Jesus is loved. . . . This, and nothing less than this is what adoption means.[14]

He loves me with the same affection He lavishes on Jesus? Is that kind of love even possible? I have pondered over the words of the apostle John with reoccurring frequency: "See how very much our Father loves us, for he calls us his children, and that is what we are." (1 John 3:1)

That truth, that kind of love, has forever reframed my world and continues to do so. As I listened, I could hear God singing over me, a sound more beautiful than the distant waves breaking on that tropical shoreline. I am no longer like the broken bottles discarded in the ocean. The discovery of God's tender Father-love is producing in me a unique beauty. Like the sea glass I relentlessly hunted on that ten-day appointment with God, imperfect and broken, I am being smoothed and reshaped by this new awareness of God's love for me.

10

A GLIMPSE OF GRACE

I remember as a college freshman sitting in a class, frustrated and put off with a paper that had been graded and returned to me. To my mind, my very scattered professor had once again shown evidence of inconsistency in his scoring. The assignment, if I remember correctly, was to write our personal story, our testimony, just as we would share it with someone who did not know Christ. My classmates who had dramatic stories, stories of near-death experiences or turbulent years of teenage rebellion, quite unfairly received A's. It seemed to me that the greater the sin, the higher the grade—quite an unfair reward for all the effort I had made to follow the rules.

And rules there were. No dancing, a rule which conjures up memories of humiliation: being singled out and sitting alone in a second- and third-grade classroom, head down on my desk with the lights turned off while my classmates square danced in the school gym. After all, "dancing could lead to impure thoughts and an unwanted pregnancy." We wouldn't want that happening to a second grader! To my young mind the hour dragged on forever as I wrestled with the shame of being different.

No movies, no exceptions! Even Billy Graham movies were banned (with one exception made in high school) if they were shown at the local cinema. I was told we would be paying for worldly movies just by darkening their doors.

And no slang? One day during recess while playing a rather competitive game of four-square, I got up my nerve, though with a great deal of trepidation, and tried out all the words I could think of that were banned from my vocabulary. To my amazement I didn't feel any different nor was I struck dead!

I did manage to deviate a bit on rules regarding dress lengths. Since my twin sister was shorter, borrowing her dresses was to my advantage; and my cleverness kept me from *actually* breaking any rules. But for all the rules I kept— and there were many—I also experienced a great deal of shame at being different from my peers at school with no resulting inner satisfaction that I was being "so good."

Not only as a child did I keep, with considerable reluctance, the rules that I was taught defined a "real" Christian; but as I grew older I also adhered to lists that defined "committed" Christians. These lists included regular devotions, door-to-door witnessing, and other disciplines that added little or no joy to my life. God seemed elusive, and I secretly wondered if God wasn't somehow indebted to me because of all my efforts to please Him.

Several months after returning from Hawaii, I read Timothy Keller's book *Prodigal God* in which he describes two kinds of "lostness" in Jesus' parable of "The Prodigal Son." Keller examines the motives of the two sons when he asks this question: What did they want most in their lives? The younger son wanted "to make his own decisions and have unfettered control of his portion of the wealth . . . a bold power play . . . a declaration of complete independence."[15] Although a stark contrast in behavior characterizes the two sons, Keller points out that the older son wanted the same thing:

> He, too, wanted the father's goods rather than the father himself. . . . His unspoken demand is, 'I have never disobeyed you! Now you have to do things in my life the way I want them to be done.'[16]

Keller sums up their relationship with their father in the following way:

> So we have two sons, one 'bad' by conventional standards and one 'good,' yet both are alienated from the father. . . . There is not just one lost son in this parable—there are two. . . . Neither son loved the father for himself. They both were using the father for their own self-centered ends rather than loving, enjoying, and serving him for his own sake. This means that you

can rebel against God and be alienated from him either by breaking his rules or by keeping all of them diligently.[17]

It was while reading this book that I had one of my many "grace-awakening" moments. In the quiet of my heart God whispered to me a thought from which grew a conviction, bringing with it a liberating freedom. It was as if He painted me into the story of "The Prodigal Son." I recognized in myself the heart of the older brother, always trying, trying to please. But what *was* my motive? As a child, did I somehow feel that God owed me a ticket to heaven because of my diligent effort to obey the moral code of conduct in my particular Christian community and family?

Now my eyes were opening to the stunning realization that in my self-righteous childhood and adolescence, I had been as lost to the Father's love as my wandering, wayward son. In fact, it took God just as much grace to save me! I cannot overstate the impact that this simple thought had on me. In the infancy of my relationship with God, I had not been motivated by love but rather by the self-righteous expectation of reward for loyal behavior, traits easily recognized in the older brother in this familiar parable.

With the passage of time, approval had unwittingly become an idol, with service to God and raising the "perfect" family being the highest forms of earned affirmation. Unfortunately, the perceived standard of perfection and service was continually being raised, or so it seemed. For a lifetime this illusive pursuit of perfection, this idol, had robbed me of the joy of knowing the Father's unconditional love.

As the years passed, I continued the vicious cycle of effort, always more effort, followed by guilt and shame that my hard work was never enough. In an attempt to earn love, I had missed love. My efforts were a weight around my soul, keeping me from looking up to see my Father's loving gaze. Although obeying many of those rules had protected me from damaging consequences as a child and adolescent—not unlike the protection it provided the "older brother," the reality was just hitting me: Being a child of God was not dependent on me. I was overwhelmed with the thought that I could not add anything to what Jesus had already done for me.

I read the words of Romans 5:8-10 as if for the first time. They clearly state that it was while I was alienated from God, while I was still a sinner, He died for me. In depending on my own works to win approval from God and others, I was actually rejecting the grace and love He offered to me. My relationship with and my position before God the Father were based on what Jesus did for me, not on what I did for Him; I could add nothing. All my attempts to please God in order to win His approval fell short. However, intuitively I longed to somehow win, to earn His love. In my mind approval and love were somehow synonymous with effort, service, and good works.

J. D. Greear's book *Gospel* gave words to my own struggle when he describes Martin Luther's assessment of this dilemma: ". . . our hearts are hard-wired for 'works righteousness'—that is, the idea that what we do determines how God feels about us."[18] An old quote by Oswald Chambers, reinforced this idea when he said, "The greatest competitor of true devotion to Jesus is the service we do for Him."[19]

Was I foolish enough to somehow believe the lie that God's approval was based on my perception of how well I was living out my faith and my service to Him? Did I perhaps believe the lie that my position with God was dependent on my attempts to earn His love rather than on a plan to which I could only respond with faith and humility, an unfathomable gift of love conceived in the heart of God that I must simply accept or reject?

I find it revealing that self-righteousness and pride are so easy to spot in another, yet these destructive roots growing deep within our own souls are so difficult to see. However, only upon its discovery, along with the awareness of my unworthiness to relate to a holy God, can I experience the wonder of grace. Strangely, it is this discovery of my own sinful self-righteousness that I cherish.

In contrast to the old mental tapes I had played that my goodness merited God's affection and love, I am attempting to rewire my thinking, to make grace my default, to allow love to grow and spill out of my life from the overflow of a heart and life saturated in the wonder of God's love for me.

Again, in the book *Gospel,* the author gives me a wonderful tool in the form of a prayer upon which to meditate. So I remind myself daily:

> *In Christ, there is nothing I can do*
> *that would make You love me more,*
> *and nothing I have done*
> *that makes You love me less.*
> *Your presence and approval*
> *are all I need for everlasting joy.*[20]

Freedom is a word too small and inadequate to describe this discovery of God's love and grace, but I am forever grateful for this journey through a difficult season of parenting. It has been the tool in God's hands to reveal His father heart to this imperfect mother with a yearning in her heart to know God more intimately.

11

EVOLUTION OF PRAYER

For as far back as I can remember prayer has been a part of my life. Not in the sense that it had considerable meaning or that God and I were really communicating, but in the sense that as a young child I had a growing awareness of my sin and its consequences. Due to the fact that I had frequent verbal spats with my twin, confession quickly became a growing part of my life.

Also, as I habitually saw answers to prayer in my parents' lives, I wanted to emulate them; so, like them, I too had a growing prayer list. I always knelt by my bed at night to pray. On numerous occasions I remember waking at 5:00 a.m., having fallen asleep once again on the hardwood floor. Cold and stiff, I was deeply disappointed that I had missed a good night of sleep in my soft, cozy bed.

As a young mother, prayer was a growing part of my life as I felt the weight of responsibility for these young sons. Although I too saw many answers to prayer, it was less than satisfying. I had great faith that God did answer prayer; however, I struggled with the belief that He genuinely liked me. Even though He responded to my faith, I had very little or no deep conviction of His personal love for me. And I must confess, my impression of what a follower of Jesus should look like was a heavy burden that tainted my view of God as well.

Despite my continuing doubts of God's love for me, as our sons' turbulent teen years rolled into our lives, I instinctively knew where to turn. In desperation I ran to God. Prayer lists were abandoned. Prayer began happening not only as a disciplined morning regimen but as a response to the choices our adolescent sons, first one, then another, were making. I was bewildered by their brazen lack of good judgment, as I had never been courageous enough myself to make choices that flew in the face of my parents' convictions.

As I became increasingly apprehensive about how to help one of our sons, God reminded me that one of His names is the "Wonderful Counselor." So to the ultimate Counselor we ran! In our desperation, my husband and I started a new routine that would become an established pattern. Each night, often between the hours of 11:00 and midnight, we would leave the house after the kids were already in bed for the night and drive a loop around our small city. Pulling over next to the river that wound its way through the center of town, we prayed for our family. Away from the commotion of a busy household, we could share our concerns with each other and with God. God had answers we did not have, so together we pleaded for His wisdom; He had made our sons and understood every motivation and every facet of their personalities.

In this perplexing season I found my prayer life driven by fear. After a restless and often short night of sleep, the peace I'd had from our late-night drives would frequently evaporate long before the new day dawned. So after dropping the kids off at school, I would head to a deserted bluff, cold and barren like my heart, overlooking the river on the edge of town.

Turning the engine off, I would place my Bible in my lap and read and re-read many of the promises God had already given me and pray them back to Him. Every ten minutes or so I would have to turn the engine back on to warm my frozen fingers and toes, continuing this routine until peace would once again warm my spirit. As I poured out my heart to God, begging for His help to navigate this complex season of my life, God not only gave me peace but also resolve. Then, and only then, would I turn the van toward home.

A subtle change was happening in me. I found that when my daily work routines distracted me and I missed those morning and evening drives, I missed being with God. I didn't have courage to face the unknown without grounding myself in the promises that He had given me, as well as in the time we shared conversing. I confess, those times with God were largely one-sided; but after a torrent of my words, fears, and requests, God, in His lovingkindness, would give me another reminder in His Word of His love for me.

The Psalms, which I had previously found depressing and dark, became my friends. Here were someone else's words adequately framing what was transpiring in my own heart. The psalmists would often conclude their frantic cries of despair with a declaration of hope in God's unfailing love and tender compassion. Steadily, yet subtly, the love of God was reshaping my vision of God, and the beauty of His promises of faithful kindness and unrelenting mercy were reshaping my prayer life. I had a growing confidence, however shaky, in God's love for our family.

In this season one book in particular had a deep impact on my badly shaken faith and life of prayer. My husband had discovered this treasure earlier—an old compilation of insights selected from Andrew Murray's classic devotional writings. Formatted as a journal, each page left room to write one's own reflections regarding the daily selection. Skimming through its pages, I knew I had to have my own copy. After searching several online used bookstores, my husband found this rare, out-of-date classic, *The Best of Andrew Murray on Prayer*, without a mark on its old pages. I cherished this gift. I felt as though I were sitting at the feet of a master, being schooled in matters of the heart that related to prayer and faith.

As I wrestled with fear, my own fledgling faith, and issues of God's timing, I would daily interact with Andrew Murray's insights by writing my own response of prayer on each page. As faith seemed to be a recurring battle for me, I knew it was essential that I trust the One to whom I prayed. With anticipation, I was hopeful that this trial of faith could, in fact, be the discovery of God. Working my way through this daily devotional journal, I was learning to trust a God who was good, powerful, and wise.

Several entries in this journal especially moved me. I related to the story in Mark 9 of a desperate father. In one momentous encounter, assertive and yet afraid, he brought his son to Jesus to heal, pleading, "Have mercy on us and help, if You can." Jesus responded to his shaky faith with a gentle rebuke, "What do you mean, 'If I can?' Anything is possible if a person believes." Mark 9:24 states, "The father instantly cried out, 'I do believe, but help me overcome my unbelief.'"

Andrew Murray offered some encouraging insights into this passage. He pointed out that Jesus not only had the power to heal the boy besieged with an evil spirit, but He also had the power to produce in the father the second miracle, "the power to inspire him with needed faith." Murray continues, "The very greatness of faith's trial was the greatness of faith's triumph."[21]

I wrote the following in my response to that devotional: "The greatness of the promise 'anything is possible' truly tests my faith. Anything? Father, my faith wavers. Like the father of that child in Mark 9, I say, 'I do believe, but help me not to doubt!'" God, in His deep compassion, looked deep into my heart and worked with the tiny faith I had. Over the months and years He has been faithfully teaching me to trust and depend on none other than Himself, the living God. Yet the greatest miracle may be that I am discovering firsthand a God who loves me and with whom I long to be, gazing with growing love not at His hands and what He can give me, but at His face.

12

GOD REMEMBERS

As time has passed, long after the initial crisis in our family, God has at times grown quiet. However, the memories of God's interventions and whisperings of love, although distant, have been forever etched in my heart and on the pages of my journal. Consequently, in those quiet seasons when I don't feel the warmth of His presence, I can turn to my record of His faithfulness and reflect on the kindness of God that is just as real today as the day He spoke those words of hope with such clarity to my quaking heart. God has reminded me often that silence does not mean abandonment. It is at such times that my faith is stretched just a bit further.

This past February I was in the midst of just such a long silent winter. I saw little or no answers to my persistent prayers. I was "knocking" yet feeling as though my words were merely echoing back with a hollowness that left me shaken. Into this cold bleak February God gave me the privilege of attending a John Piper conference in Minneapolis with my husband. Numerous sessions gave me direction and challenged me concerning ministry, but none addressed the feeling of emptiness in my heart.

On the last morning of the conference I felt compelled to pray a very unusual prayer. I had seen the author's name, Sam Storms, listed on the schedule of speakers. As his book, *The Singing God*, had deeply impacted me on those quiet mornings in Hawaii some years ago, I wanted to meet him and share briefly with him the profound impact his book had left on me.

Much to my disappointment, although he was in attendance that last morning, I noticed he would not be speaking; he was merely there to address a group concerning a ministry in which he was involved. I was further discouraged with the logistical improbability of tracking him down among hundreds of pastors filling the conference center. I prayed a quick prayer early that morning, flinging up to God the brief thought that if I inadvertently ran into Sam Storms, I would share with him how God had used him in my life.

The last morning passed uneventfully. As the final session ended, we joined a sea of conferees headed back to our impressive downtown hotel. We planned to grab a quick lunch before catching our shuttle bus to the airport. As we passed a distinguished-looking gentleman sitting in the lobby, my husband turned to me and said, "That is Sam Storms; you really ought to introduce yourself and tell him how much his book encouraged you." I was stunned! I hadn't told my husband of my early morning prayer. But the thought of approaching a complete stranger was quite intimidating, so I kept walking.

As we headed toward the revolving door that would take us out to the street, my husband repeated his suggestion. I knew then that I needed to follow through on this God-orchestrated opportunity. Although my encounter with this author and speaker was brief and I stumbled to share with any clarity the book's impact on me, I was touched by the reminder of God's love and presence. He was still with me! Waiting and silence does not equal abandonment.

I recently ran across an obscure but compelling verse in Micah 7:7 in which the prophet declares his confidence in God when he states, "As for me, I look to the LORD for help. I wait confidently for God to save me, and my God will certainly hear me." There seems to be a pattern of faith woven throughout Scripture that I am inexplicably drawn to: men and women of faith, in the midst of trials and silence, who still remain confident that God, in fact, hears those who wait on Him.

This season has provided the impetus that has driven my unfolding discovery of a God who loves me. I am humbled and grateful for these unexpected touches of grace upon my life. They have deepened my confidence that He will indeed hear me even when I am faced with prolonged silence. This growing confidence has, in turn, nurtured my love for Him.

13

GOD'S STORMS

I am one of many in our church family who have committed to reading through the Bible this year in the *Gospel Transformation Bible.* From the beginning of Genesis and throughout its pages, I have been struck by the way God intersects the lives of a very flawed humanity.

There is Abraham, his faith unshaken even when asked to surrender his cherished son to a plan that required unprecedented faith. His faith would inspire believers for generations. There is Jacob, a strong, controlling man who wrestled with God and was marked forever by God with a limp. That limp would symbolize a life brought into dependence upon Him and a life through which God's grace would be displayed. But it is Joseph that has mesmerized and captured my thoughts.

Joseph: a cocky, young boy who raised the ire of his brothers by flaunting his father's favoritism, which he relished. Joseph: taunting his brothers with dreams that predicted their subjection to him. Joseph: who must have cried with panic from a pit as he realized he had pushed them too far. Joseph: sold into slavery by jealous brothers to a caravan of traders from another country. Joseph: fearing to never again see his father who passionately, yet unwisely, loved him with preferential treatment. And Joseph: crushed by the weight of betrayal, his young life spinning out of control. His world had seemingly ended. This young man's future was, to the human mind, cut short. Even God's covenant promise to Abraham to use this family to bless the nations seemed thwarted.

As I read the account of Joseph's life from the pages of Genesis, I was deeply moved, being in the throes of a betrayal of my own. Like Joseph who basked in the warmth of his father's preferential love even while the clouds of family tensions were building on the horizon, I too was feeling the joy of God's presence and love washing over me in this lengthy and protracted season of raising teenagers, unaware of another conflict looming on our horizon. Just as Joseph was caught off-guard by the fury of his brothers' hatred, I also felt ill-prepared for the new storm that was brewing of a completely different nature, a storm that gave few warning signs as to its impending intensity.

This storm blew in from a different and unanticipated direction. It blindsided me and left me dazed. It was a storm brought on by the betrayal of a co-worker with whom I had served side by side, someone I loved and to whom I had opened my heart. My illusion of ministry being relatively safe was destroyed. How could someone I counted as a friend and fellow servant of Jesus turn and attack with a vicious intensity that, to me, seemed almost surreal? I was staggered by the influence this individual had even with people whom I counted as friends.

I had barely gotten my feet under me; my confidence in God was growing, but still shaky. I felt unequipped for this peculiar type of suffering. The knot in my stomach returned as I faced the desertion of friends and acquaintances alike, and I asked myself daily how I could ever trust again.

I penned the following words on a sleepless night as I was made aware of the betrayal that rocked my world:

> Nothing prepared me for the accusations and the gossip leveled against us I have picked up from emails and the tidbits of talk I am hearing from others. I am shaken to the core and deeply wounded by these accusations and insinuations about our character.

I was crushed. It was devastating and humiliating to have my name and reputation brought into question. Words were used to describe me that haunt me to this day. I was reeling with the awareness that no one even asked or seemed to care if the stories swirling around my life were remotely true. No accuser would step forward. The accusations came in the form of senseless gossip. The betrayal was made worse by those who believed these stories, but worse yet was the inevitable piling on and the cheap shots that were taken.

However, the accusers remained resolutely unwilling to meet with us, as if they had vanished from our lives but not from the lives of those around us. There was no apparent desire or willingness to reconcile, leaving me vulnerable to the ongoing winds of criticism that swirled around our lives. I was left with an unresolved conflict and a wake of damage to assess and attempt to repair with the people they had influenced.

I sought to make sense of the animosity unleashed upon us. To my finite mind it did not have to happen this way. Not unlike Joseph, I felt the crushing weight of rejection by a number of people I had counted as friends. *Crushing*—a word that surfaced time and again as I sorted through a wide range of emotions.

Isaiah 41:10 states: "Don't be afraid, for I am with you." A friend and mentor in whom we confided encouraged us with these familiar words spoken in Isaiah 43:2 where God promises His presence:

> When you pass through the waters, *I will be with you*; and through the rivers, they shall not overwhelm you; when you walk through fire you shall not be burned, and the flame shall not consume you. (ESV, emphasis mine)

I spent several days reminding myself of these four simple but profound words, "I am with you." There was not one situation I was walking into alone; He was there *with* me, by my side.

Joseph was sold into slavery, betrayed by his siblings. In the unfolding of Genesis 39, as I witnessed this young man being elevated to a place of prominence and power in Egypt, I repeatedly read the statement, "The LORD was *with* Joseph (v. 2, ESV) . . . the LORD was *with* him." (v. 3, ESV) At the end of the chapter I read the account of Joseph once more being unjustly taken into captivity, this time the victim of false allegations. Yet there, too, were the words, "But the LORD was *with* Joseph and showed him steadfast love" (v. 21, ESV) and again in verse 23, "The LORD was *with* him." (ESV) God was *with* him in the storm that had become his life. (emphases mine)

My husband, who saw and witnessed my rawness, shared with me a quote by Amy Carmichael that has played often in my thoughts:

> But God is the God of the waves and the billows, and they are still *His* when they come over us; and again and again we have proved that the overwhelming thing does not overwhelm.[22]

An even more profound thought was taking hold in my mind. God was not only *with* me in these confusing and messy circumstances in which we found ourselves, He was *in* them. He is *in* the storms of my life. How can the very thing that overwhelms me not overwhelm? I am increasingly convinced that the answer lies in trusting God's sovereignty and His power to control the details of my life—that He is, in fact, *in* them. I came across an excerpt by Jerry Bridges affirming that God indeed is in control: "Nothing is so small or too trivial as to escape the attention of God's sovereign control; nothing is so great as to be beyond His power to control."[23]

Approximately two decades passed before Joseph again laid eyes on the very ones who callously and maliciously betrayed him. His brothers had come to Egypt seeking assistance for the drought that was devastating their homeland. As they bowed humbly before him, oblivious to his identity, Joseph finally revealed himself to his brothers. Professing his belief in the sovereignty of God, Joseph states, "So it was not you who sent me here, but God." (Genesis 45:8, ESV)

How could he declare with such confidence the sovereignty of God? By all appearances he had been abandoned by God, and others had seemingly controlled his destiny. Joseph recognized that ultimately it was not his brothers who were in control of his life, but God. He had learned to trust a God who was hidden yet very much present. With eyes of faith he could see that God had not only allowed the storm that was his life, He was *in* it. God was preparing Joseph and setting the stage for him to preserve his family and to fulfill God's covenant promise to His people.

In the early morning hours as sleep eluded me, I read from Psalm 138:8, "The LORD will fulfill His purpose for me; your steadfast love, O LORD, endures forever." (ESV) God's purposes for me will not be thwarted. In the midst of our pain, as life feels like it is unraveling, God is very much *with* us and *in* each painful circumstance. Life's weights are sometimes crushing, surfacing from a myriad of unexpected directions, but they cannot crush God's purposes toward us or obliterate his unwavering love for us. In truth, they are God's tools to shape us and fit us for the good purposes He has planned for us.

With gentle sensitivity my sister shared with me the words of Paul who knew to a far greater degree than I what it meant to be crushed. Through this crushing, Paul passionately exhorts the Corinthians to see their varied and sometimes overwhelming trials as opportunities to reflect Christ:

> We now have this light shining in our hearts, but we ourselves are like fragile clay jars containing this great treasure. This makes it clear that our great power is from God, not from ourselves. We are pressed on every side by troubles, but we are not crushed. We are perplexed, but not driven to despair. We are hunted down, but never abandoned by God. We get knocked down, but we are not destroyed. Through suffering, our bodies continue to share in the death of Jesus so that the life of Jesus may also be seen in our bodies. (2 Corinthians 4:7-10)

Paul recognized that the greatest gift he could give the Corinthians was to inspire them, not with his strength or even his own resilience in bouncing back under pressure and persecution, but rather with the revelation that it was the life and power of Christ shining through his weakness.

Likewise, it is through crushing that I have the opportunity to honor Him by choosing to trust Him when I do not understand His plans for me. Whether in the confusion of navigating through the various stresses of parenting, in the storms of messy relationships and unresolved conflict, or in the various trials I have yet to experience living on this flawed and broken planet, I can choose to trust my heavenly Father.

My oldest son's little girl, on her very hard two-year-old days, sometimes says to her daddy as he comes through their back door from work, "Daddy, I'm fragile!" We laugh; but I mirror those words to my Father as I acknowledge my human frailty. With that acknowledgement comes the recognition that my weakness provides the opportunity for Christ's life to be witnessed in this fragile human vessel as He works out His purposes for and in me.

14

I REMEMBER

When I was young in my faith and read verses that included instructions to "always give thanks" and to "be joyful," I would find myself obediently saying the appropriate words. However, my heart was not deceived. I was *not* thankful for trials and hardships, and no amount of effort could conjure up those kinds of emotions. Why would God require me to play these mind games that were not a reflection of my heart anyway? Yes, I knew that through this discipline of thanksgiving character could be developed, but this was not a satisfying nor a strong enough motivation for me.

Yet as God has unveiled His grace before my eyes, discovering gratitude has become a natural outcome. I have felt His grace in the touch of friends and family, in miracles along the way, and, most significantly, in the personal revealing of His own love for me. Intentional reflection on these kindnesses of God to me amidst the trials and testings of the past decade has replaced a disciplined, contrived plan of actively pursuing gratitude.

Disciplined gratitude, if I may call it that, can be accomplished with positive, although inadequate, results. Even when I have listed the many touches of God's grace upon my life, my heart seems to drift back to a restlessness that needs to be anchored in something deeper and more profound than any courageous discipline on my part. I am not suggesting that remembering is a mere sentimental attachment to the past. I am speaking of a remembering that is grounded in the faithfulness of God in the past and points me forward to a hope in God for my present and future.

When I was a child, while my beloved grandfather lay dying in our guest bedroom, he would often have me read to him from the Psalms. Shortly before his death he had me read a psalm I found quite peculiar—Psalm 106, a psalmist's historical accounting of the Israelites' wayward journeying from God. To my young mind Psalm 23 seemed much more fitting than this dry history of Israel's failures. Yet the reading of this psalm was one of his dying requests. When I finished reading, my grandfather looked so peaceful, so serene. I did not understand as I had not been similarly moved, and it left me deeply perplexed, though intrigued.

I am only now beginning to understand. Recently I read my own journaling, my accounting of God's faithfulness. Here in my own history, in my journey with God, I was deeply moved by the magnitude of God's undeserved kindness. How often my faith had lapsed or I had simply not made God my "one thing" in life, that one passion that had consumed the psalmist's life, spoken of in Psalm 27:4, where he eloquently spoke of his longing to live in God's presence, caught up with His beauty. Unlike the psalmist, there were times I had pulled away from God, deserving His hand of correction. But instead of treating me as I deserved, God revealed His faithful love.

In those moving moments before my grandfather's death, I wonder if perhaps he was reflecting on God's faithfulness to him, on his history with God. Was he thinking back to how God had brought him to America on a ship at the age of sixteen with only an older brother as his companion? Or maybe he was recalling that move to a desolate eastern Montana prairie where he would meet a rancher who would share his faith in Christ with this young immigrant. Or perhaps it was God's faithfulness and provision he pondered as he remembered moving his large, young family to northwestern Montana to homestead after losing his farm in the devastation of the Great Depression. Were those moments of reading the history of Israel for him an accounting, a reckoning of God's faithfulness and kindness?

Why do I so quickly forget God? Jerry Bridges points out in his book, *Trusting God*, that it is man's inclination and bent not to see God's hand in our lives, even as Paul states in Romans 1:1: "Although they knew God, they did not honor him as God or give thanks to him." (ESV) Bridges asserts that "our problem is far deeper than mere forgetfulness. We are imbued with a spirit of ingratitude because of our sinful nature. We must cultivate a new spirit, the spirit of gratitude." How can I do that without it becoming another mechanical work of the flesh? Jerry Bridges answers my question with this statement: "Thanksgiving is an admission of dependence."[24]

As I freely acknowledge that my heart is prone to wander, remembering is a tool to instruct and guide my heart, teaching me to live in submission and dependence on my God. Remembering points me to a history filled with His compassion and faithfulness, enabling me with abandon to make Him my "one thing."

However, within life there are those moments when rejoicing, giving thanks, and even remembering seem incompatible, if not contradictory, with the circumstances in which we find ourselves. Tim Keller's book, *Walking with God through Pain and Suffering*, has been a recent companion during some dark, sleepless nights of my own as I have tried to make sense of the storms that accompany serving a broken world. Keller maintains that weathering the pain and suffering of life is not a call to toughness nor is it a "self-absorbed, self-sufficient response."[25] We are not called to inaccurately remember, assessing our suffering with a denial of the pain and hurt we feel in life. Rather, joy can be found *within* sorrow.

How can joy and inner turmoil of the soul be compatible? Can I be grateful and weep? Can I rejoice and see a God of love through my tears? Does rejoicing mean the absence of uncomfortable emotions? Can—and *should*—those troublesome emotions simply be turned off?

Tim Keller goes on to explain in the following statement:

> To 'rejoice' in God means to dwell on and remind ourselves of who God is, who we are, and what he has done for us. Sometimes our emotions respond and follow when we do this, and sometimes they do not . . . we must not define rejoicing as something that precludes feelings of grief, or doubt, weakness, and pain. Rejoicing in suffering happens within sorrow. . . . The grief and sorrow drive you more into God.[26]

Throughout his book I felt as if I were being schooled by the examples of Biblical characters and contemporaries alike. Their stories and personal histories are unique, yet curiously similar, as they discovered God in the storms of their lives. Not unlike my grandfather, as I ponder my own story of walking with God, gratitude is born in me as well. Through intentional remembering, I remind myself of who God is, who I am, and what He has done for me and in me.

The study notes on Deuteronomy 2:1-25 in the *ESV Gospel Transformation Bible* call this remembering "motivational history."[27] The commentator points out the following:

> The recitation of covenant history in Deuteronomy 1-4 is a means to an end. The *end* is motivation to live by the teachings found in Deuteronomy 5-26. The

means is reminding the covenant people of the grace that God had granted them in the past by His promises, provision, and deliverance. (emphases mine)

He goes on to conclude, ". . . obedience to God's teachings is always to be motivated by what God has graciously done for us in the past."[28]

My own motivational history is a record of God's hand in the details of my life. There are the times I have opened the Bible and been profoundly touched by a truth. And there are the little miracles that show God's interaction in the details of my life, like the "coincidental" phone calls or texts from an encouraging friend. An unforced gratitude and confidence in God has grown as I have reflected on my personal history and how God has graciously dealt with me in my past. Remembering these fingerprints of God on my life is for me a backward glance that gives me a future hope, keeping me connected with a God of love and grace.

The ultimate remembering takes me back time and time again to the cross, that pivotal point in history when the Father turned His back on His Son and gave Him up to face the punishment that I deserve, treating Him as a sinner. Why? God's fierce love offered to pay a debt I could not satisfy, as stated in 2 Corinthians 5:21: "For God made Christ, who never sinned, to be the offering for our sin, so that we could be made right with God through Christ." I am offered a relationship with God because of His fierce love. The unfolding of

God's love in Christ is, to me, truly motivational history. And when all else seems dark, I still have a solid reason to rejoice!

15

AN UNEXPECTED GIFT

Although it was only mid-April, I got the crazy idea to clean out my gardens. They were a mass of dead leaves and dry, brittle stalks that once held lovely perennials. These hardy plants must weather not only harsh spring and autumn winds gusting upward of 50 mph, but also winters that can dip to 30 degrees below zero, accompanied by snow that buries my once-struggling flower gardens. I am not a gardener by nature, but I do love beautiful flower gardens—an important distinction! Despite all my efforts, my gardens never quite develop into the exquisite and thriving masterpieces I envision, but in the spring I am always hopeful once again.

As we were expecting snow again the next day and the following month I had a schedule that looked difficult to manage, I headed out to tackle my unsightly gardens littered with garbage and every manner of debris that blows up our street. I do not look forward to this yearly task. I was rather pessimistic as, little by little over the years,

I have grown disheartened by my ambitious ideas and disappointing results.

I dragged myself outside, limping as I moved, since I had only a month ago undergone foot surgery. My spirits and body were lagging, but the sunshine pulled me outdoors. I told myself it would be good for me.

As I began the dirty task of cutting the dead stalks and clearing the decaying leaves, I was delighted to see little green shoots peeking through. What appeared on the surface to be dead was throbbing with renewed life. Although I only planned to tackle one flowerbed, I found myself pushing on, looking for more signs of life. Not every plant encouraged me with tender green sprouts; but early spring hope is infectious and I imagined, in only a few short months, delicate pink flowers on my new bleeding heart bush, along with yellow daylilies and purple salvia filling my garden.

Limping my way back to the house, I entered dirty, stiff, and sore, yet satisfied. Just as my flower gardens showed signs of promise, I am also hopeful about my life. There have been moments in the past decade when it appeared as if my dreams had all been mere wishes. Hope had evaporated, and it had been hard to remember the beauty that filled my life. My heart had felt frozen, not unlike the dormant flowers in my untended gardens. Yet, like my awakening perennials, life and hope are still there.

I have discovered, even in my most barren seasons, the faithfulness of God. Although at times my heart has felt parched and withered with little or no signs of life, God has never let my longing for Him die. Rather than a god who is distant or condemning, I have instead experienced a God who loves me. He surprises me with His gentle touches through miracles, friends, and quiet whispering in the darkest midnights. It is a journey too valuable to resent or to complain about. His fierce love holds me fast.

Working my way through the Old Testament, I read the story of Esther, a young Jewish girl exiled from her homeland. She was thrust into a plan orchestrated by God to preserve His people from a power-hungry, conniving servant of the king of Persia. Esther's own cousin Mordecai became victim to an evil plot to destroy the remnant of Jews in exile in this vast territory. Her life must have felt out of control. She alone, elevated to the position of queen, had the power to save not only her cousin, but all her people as well.

But this plan was not without risks; it could have cost her very life. The uneasiness and fear with which Esther met this challenge were entirely human. Esther, together with her servants, turned to God, the only One who could save them. Her humble dependence on God enabled her to face with courage the king who held her life in his hands.

Like Esther, there are times when I feel that I'm in over my head. It is hard to see with any confidence the purposes in the plan and scope of my life. It is above me. It is hard to have hope and courage. In these moments God reminds me of His promise in James 4:10, "Get down on your knees before the Master; it's the only way you'll get on your feet." (MSG) Just as Mordecai asked Esther to go before the king, God invites me to come humbly before Him; He graciously grants His favor and honor so His purposes can be accomplished.

The story of Esther reminds me of a phrase by Jared Wilson in his book *Gospel Wakefulness*, a phrase that I have turned over in my mind with recurring frequency these past few years. He speaks of a "gospel confidence,"[29] a confidence in God's love and grace that produces both humility and boldness, traits easily recognizable in the life of Esther.

I have looked for signs of these two graces growing in me while my heart has gradually thawed after this bleak season and has been warmed by an awakening of His grace. As I have been broken by the circumstances in my life, by my own misconceptions of God, and by the expectations of others, I have been humbled. As I have been broken of my need for approval, I have been emboldened by God's forgiveness and love, a love I could not earn. Because God's kindness and love are not dependent upon me, I am free to admit my limitations. I am free from a need to impress. I am free to be honest, for I am growing in the confidence of who God declares me to be. I am now walking with what I can only call a confident limp.

I love how Timothy Keller sums up this concept in the following:

The Christian gospel is that I am so flawed that Jesus had to die for me, yet I am so loved and valued that Jesus was glad to die for me. This leads to deep humility and deep confidence at the same time. It undermines both swaggering and sniveling. I cannot feel superior to anyone, and yet I have nothing to prove to anyone.[30]

God's love emboldens me with a growing awareness that the outcome of my life does not just rest on my shoulders, but ultimately on His. Nothing can separate me from His love, not my spotty performance in all the roles that encompass my life nor the outside influences in the human and spirit worlds. As I contemplate the beauty of His faithful love, these paradoxical graces of humility and confidence are slowly being birthed in me. They are unexpected gifts in my journey into grace.

16

FULL CIRCLE

I am sitting here at a dining room table in a 1960s-style condo, looking out over a beautiful mountain lake. Three years ago, in this same condo complex, I first began my attempts at sorting through my thoughts and deciphering what God was whispering to my heart through this confusing season. Countless words have been scratched out on random sheets of paper over these past three years, and it has taken a great deal of diligence to collect my thoughts and attempt to express them with any clarity. But I am not the same person I was ten years ago or even three years ago. I have been indelibly marked by my journey into God's grace. However, that does not exempt me from the daily challenges and from people who defy my newfound freedom.

Is there someone in your life with a great deal of power over how you see yourself? Someone you dread connecting with or someone who could push you into therapy after only a few short hours together? I have a confession to make—and I am sure I am not the only one who immediately had a face or faces pop into their mind! I have such a person who has had that kind of powerful impact on me. For weeks before she arrives, I dread seeing her; and in the not-so-distant past I would be devastated for weeks after she left. She has the ability to point out all my imperfections: my housekeeping is not quite good enough, the food I prepare isn't healthy enough, and my children, she presumes, aren't as smart as her own. Sadly, all this is said with a pleasant smile on her face!

I wonder if we Christians sometimes use a smiling persona to nullify our thoughtless words and justify our own insecurities. I am convinced that these tense exchanges could have been somewhat alleviated if she would only have shown an interest in my harried life or maybe have offered a kind word of gratitude with a bit more frequency. But I am now more aware than ever that there is an alternative to letting others define me.

When I started this arduous journey, I regrettably received my worth from people and voices, including my own, who defined me by my performance in all the areas that mattered deeply to me: my marriage, my parenting, my service to God, and on and on the list goes. Although I am daily discovering the beauty of what it means to be loved by a God who far surpasses any hopes and dreams I had for my relationship with Him, I find I am still not immune to this struggle of who and what determine my value. The deeply ingrained habits and voices I listen to must continually be reckoned with. As I hear God's persuading voice gently reaffirming His love for me through His Word, I find the opinions and criticisms of others have a diminishing power over me. There is a growing peace deep within my soul that enables me to handle the voices I once entertained in my search for the acceptance and love I craved.

I am reading *Crash the Chatterbox* by Steven Furtick during this week of study, and the author has much to say about listening to the voices in our minds and replacing them with God's truth. I see myself in some of his descriptions, especially in the one that follows: "You're spending too much energy assessing other people's assessment of you. I want you to reinvest that energy into aligning your life with My acceptance of you."[31]

What a fitting picture this is of my journey: silencing my own voice as well as the voices of others as I seek to hear and define myself by God's truth. Unfortunately, we live and breathe in a world where we are constantly being bombarded by voices that distort the truth God speaks over us.

Upon a recent reading of the book of Job, I saw this conflict of voices lived out. I found myself fascinated and even angry at the role Job's misguided "righteous" friends played. They only served to intensify Job's spiritual anguish with their many words in the midst of his trial of most epic proportions. To their finite minds Job's suffering must be analyzed so as to explain the severity of the trial. Their heated dialogue with Job, which comprises much of this Old Testament book, is an attempt to fix his life so that his pain will be alleviated.

But what if exposing a particular sin was not the purpose of this trial God allowed to encompass Job's life? What if his friends were wrong and the purpose of the trial was not punitive?

I am equally fascinated by the candor and boldness with which Job speaks to God. It is not unlike David's brash questioning of the Almighty when in Psalm 13:1, 2 he cries out:

> O LORD, how long will you forget me? Forever? How long will you look the other way? How long must I struggle with anguish in my soul, with sorrow in my heart every day? How long will my enemy have the upper hand?

Why did God not cut short this torrent of seemingly defiant words challenging God's perfect character expressed by both Job and David? Why did God defend Job even though he was guilty of bitter complaints and a wavering faith? Timothy Keller, in his book *Walking with God through Pain and Suffering,* points out that it is first because God is a gracious and forgiving God. However, notice what he points out about Job's posture before God:

> . . . the crucial thing to notice is this: Through it all, Job never stopped praying. Yes, he complained. . . . He doubted. . . . He screamed and yelled, but he did it in God's presence. He kept seeking Him. . . . Job's doggedness in seeking the face and presence of God meant that the suffering did

not drive him away from God but toward Him.[32]

On the surface it is presumptuous to compare myself with Job, but I am fascinated by his raw honesty and his spirited, even challenging, exchanges with God. His meritorious view of God resonates with me: We perform well, live "righteously," and God does His part by blessing us and keeping us from trials and pain. Isn't that how it's supposed to work? No. And that's one of the main points of the book of Job.

God used this most undeserved trial to strip Job of any expectation of earning God's favor and reward simply through a godly life. Instead, he was driven into God. In Keller's words:

> He retracts his demand that God . . . must give him explanation and public vindication. He gives up trying to control God. . . . He bows before God and lets him be who he is. He serves God for himself alone.[33]

God does not answer all of Job's questions directly but instead gives him the gift of Himself, of knowing Him more fully through their candid and frank dialogue. His bravado is gone as he aligns his heart with God's, surrendering to God's judgments rather than his own. He acknowledges in Job 42:1 that God can do anything and that none of His plans can be frustrated. In verse five of this chapter, Job's understanding has now moved from his head to his heart when he declares, "My ears had heard of you but now my eyes have seen you." (NIV) He has become, as Francis Anderson so richly states, "the companion of God."[34]

As I look back at these past ten years I see a shift, a change of trajectory. I don't know why it took so long for the beauty of the gospel to move from my head to my heart, so long to hear God's voice. Perhaps it's because I knew more facts about the Bible and God than I was forced to live. I confess I lived somewhat independently of God, using Him, as it were, for the emergencies and the goals which I deemed worthy and virtuous. My ears were more attuned to the voices of others, and my own demanding needs overshadowed the quiet voice of God calling to me.

In the words of C. S. Lewis, these years have been for me "a severe mercy."[35] The fears, losses, and unanswered prayers I most dreaded became the very tools that God used to painfully strip me of "me," leaving me vulnerable in His presence. Even so, He never left me. In my vulnerability, fighting down the shame that had plagued me for a lifetime, God began to reveal to me that I was deeply loved and cherished by none other than Almighty God Himself. I am extravagantly and lavishly loved. How exceedingly grateful I am for this journey into grace.

Laura Story poignantly describes the beauty of this discovery in the midst of pain in the song she penned called "Blessings." Her ending words have become my own, and I have sung them many nights during my drive home from work. They are

a beautiful expression of God's hand in the midst
of our pain:

> *What if my greatest disappointments*
> *Or the aching of this life*
> *Is the revealing of a greater thirst*
> *This world can't satisfy?*
> *What if trials of this life—*
> *The rain, the storms, the hardest nights,*
> *Are your mercies in disguise?*[36]

I am grateful for these "mercies in disguise."
Through these storms I have heard His voice
of love, and His is ultimately the only voice that
matters.

Almost three years to the day have passed
since I began writing down these musings. As I sit
on this balcony overlooking the beauty of the
valley bathed in light peeking through the summer
rainclouds, it is with a peculiar fondness I am
thanking God for this journey. There is something
more important than having all my questions
answered: It is to know and be known by Him. I
would never have understood or felt His fierce,
extravagant love if it were not for this "severe
mercy."

ENDNOTES

2 PREPARATION...

1 Martin Luther, cited by Jim Cymbala, *The Promise of Answered Prayer* (Grand Rapids: Zondervan, 2003), p. 140.

2 Ron Mehl, *Surprise Endings* (Portland: Multnomah, 1995), pp. 72-74.

3 PROMISES . . . AND WAITING

3 Jim Cymbala, *The Life God Blesses* (Grand Rapids: Zondervan, 2001), pp. 140-141.

4 BROKENNESS

4 Ravi Zacharias, *The Grand Weaver* (Grand Rapids: Zondervan, 2010), pp. 39-40.

5 Jared Wilson, *Gospel Wakefulness* (Wheaton: Crossway, 2011), p. 24.

6 Ibid., p. 35.

7 Ibid., p. 39.

8 Ibid., p. 41.

5 DARKNESS

9 Martyn Lloyd-Jones cited by Jared C. Wilson, *Gospel Wakefulness* (Wheaton: Crossway, 2011), p. 156.

10 John Stott cited by Jared C. Wilson, *Gospel Wake-fulness,* p. 161.

7 DOUBTS

11 Sanctus Real, "Whatever You're Doing" (Something Heavenly), from *We Need Each Other,* Birdwing Music, 2008, compact disc.

9 HAWAII

[12] J. I. Packer cited by Sam Storms, *The Singing God* (Lake Mary, FL: Charisma House, 2013), p. 48.

[13] Sam Storms, *The Singing God*, p. 49.

[14] Ibid., p. 50.

10 A GLIMPSE OF GRACE

[15] Timothy Keller,*The Prodigal God* (London: Penguin Books, 2011), p. 35.

[16] Ibid., p. 36.

[17] Ibid., pp. 34, 35, 36.

[18] Martin Luther cited by J. D. Greear, *Gospel* (Nash-ville: B&H Books, 2011), p. 48.

[19] Oswald Chambers, *My Utmost for His Highest*, January 18.

[20] Greear, *Gospel*, p. 44.

11 EVOLUTION OF PRAYER

[21] Edward A. Elliott, comp., *The Best of Andrew Murray on Prayer* (Uhrichsville: Barbour Publishing, 1998), p. 23.

13 GOD'S STORMS

[22] Amy Carmichael, cited by William Edgar, *Schaeffer on the Christian Life: Countercultural Spirituality* (Wheaton: Crossway, 2013), p. 125.

[23] Jerry Bridges, *Trusting God*, cited by *How Great is Our God, Timeless Daily Readings on the Nature of God* (Carol Stream: NavPress, 2011), p. 77.

14 I REMEMBER

[24] Jerry Bridges, *Trusting God*, cited in *How Great is Our God, Timeless Daily Readings on the Nature of God*, p. 309.

[25] Timothy Keller, *Walking with God through Pain and Suffering* (London: Penguin Books, 2015), p. 252.

26 Ibid., p. 253.

27 ESV Gospel Transformation Bible, p. 221.

28 Ibid., p. 221.

15 AN UNEXPECTED GIFT

29 Jared Wilson, *Gospel Wakefulness* (Wheaton: Crossway Books, 2011), p. 170.

30 Timothy Keller, *The Reason for God*, cited by Jared C. Wilson, *Gospel Wakefulness*, p. 171.

16 FULL CIRCLE

31 Steven Furtick, *Crash the Chatterbox* (Colorado Springs: Multnomah Books, 2015), p. 31.

32 Timothy Keller, *Walking with God through Pain and Suffering* (London: Penguin Books, 2015), pp. 287, 288.

33 Ibid., p. 292.

34 Francis Anderson cited by Timothy Keller, *Walking with God through Pain and Suffering*, p. 293.

35 Sheldon Vanauken, *A Severe Mercy* (New York: Harper & Row, 1977), p. 211.

36 Laura Story, "Blessings," from *Blessings*, Columbia, 2011, compact disc.

Made in the USA
Las Vegas, NV
03 June 2022

49754959R00068